THE ENTERTAINERS
TONY HANCOCK

Other books by Philip Oakes

Novels
Exactly What We Want
The God Botherers
Experiment at Proto

Poetry
Unlucky Jonah
In the Affirmative
Married/Singular

The Entertainers
Edited by Philip Oakes

TONY HANCOCK

Philip Oakes

Woburn-Futura

First published in Great Britain in 1975 by Woburn-Futura
110 Warner Road, London S.E.5

Copyright © Philip Oakes 1975

ISBN 0 7130 0138 0

Printed in Great Britain by Butler & Tanner Ltd, Frome and London

Designed by Gilvrie Misstear

Picture Credits

Associated Press 93
BBC 7, 14–15, 32–33, 35, 38–39, 42–43, 61, 64–65, 68–69
Mike Busselle 41
Camera Press 22
Cartier Bresson (John Hillelson Agency) 81
British Film Institute back cover, 56–57, 58–59, 78–79
British Rail 54–55
Peter Brough 11, 27
Egg Marketing Board 89
Ronald Grant 8
Julie Hamilton 87
London Express News & Features Service 47
Philip Oakes 74–75
Robert Penn/Associated British Film Picture Corp. Ltd 37
Popperfoto 12, 20, 28, 29, 48, 49, 50–51, 52, 71, 77, 88, 90
Private Eye 19
Radio Times 17, 44

Picture research by Lynette Trotter

The name of the game

On his bad days, which were many, Tony Hancock felt persecuted by his own name. You'd see him wince when an admirer, spotting him across a crowded bar, would nail him with a shout and head towards him, hands poised to pound the celebrated shoulders. And Hancock, who hated to be touched, would nerve himself for the ordeal; a commodity flinching from the point of sale.

It was not what he had ever intended. The name had become a label. He'd worked hard to make it famous, but seeing it in lights, hearing himself hailed ("Like a taxi," he said), made him feel like public property. At those moments Hancock longed to become invisible; only fleetingly at first, as rich men in their cups crave nostalgically to be poor once more. And usually the moment would pass. He was no one's fool. He was not above "using the name", as he put it, to secure the best table in a restaurant, to wrest special service from a hall porter. But he used it sparingly like a charm, to be uttered only in times of real need.

He was awed by its power and by the fact that, for millions of people, it represented one person only; the hero of East Cheam, the Lad himself. It was not fame that he found intolerable but the weight of fiction it entailed. Fiction, what's more, in which he had collaborated and which he feared had come to possess him utterly.

The public Hancock was not really him, he insisted. He was not the bombastic, seedy, pretentious, rhetorical, cunning, highpowered mug projected by his best-ever scriptwriters, Alan Simpson and Ray Galton. *Their* Hancock, he claimed, was based on random aspects of his true personality, as distant from what he'd become as the Ghost of Christmas Past. And desperately he tried to sever his substance from their shadow.

All in vain. For fifteen years he was, beyond all doubt, the most popular, the most successful, the most original, and the best-loved comedian in Britain. His radio and television series enjoyed top ratings. He was acclaimed by social theorists as "a massive caricature of mid-century man" (a title he rather liked). Harold Macmillan, the

Prime Minister of the day, complained that affairs of state denied him hours of telly-viewing with Hancock in view. He was a favourite not only of the groundlings but of the Royal Family and he performed privately at Windsor Castle ("A very nice class of audience," he was wont to remark). He created some of the finest, funniest, most durable comedy of the century. But in the summer of 1968 he took his own life and few of those who knew him were even faintly surprised.

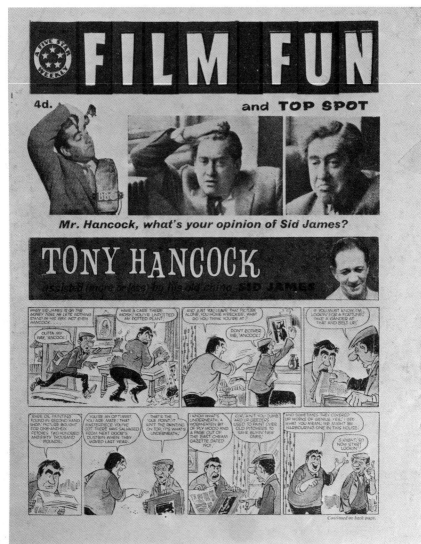

Funny things happen

What's remarkable is that, given the tragic circumstances of Hancock's death – an overdose of barbiturates washed down by vodka in a Sydney flat – there's no worm of nostalgia nibbling at his reputation. On record, on tape, and in print he remains a belligerently funny man: a positive life force.

He detested pathos. He despised comics who fell down for a laugh and homespun philosophers who dispensed sentiment in half-pound jars. He declared frequently that comedy was pain, a ceaseless probing for the truth. And while he was decidedly rough on those who worked with him, he was hardest on himself.

It is no idle phrase to speak now of 'post-Hancock comedy'. He showed what could be done by both writers and performers if they were sufficiently dedicated. And the lessons have been absorbed. Even during his lifetime he had his imitators, all of whom he watched critically as they went through their paces – usually on TV – noting their form and their potential, resenting the fact that they could practise their professional larceny without acknowledgment.

But, of course, Hancock himself had his masters and he was not above borrowing from them. About Chaplin he had reservations. The Tramp and The Little Fellow were not for him. He disliked their sentimentality and their calculated appeal. But Chaplin's ruthlessness, the zest with which he would dispatch a rival with a boot in the stomach, won his approval. He cared little for Harry Langdon, whose doughy visage with its saucer eyes reminded him of a mental defective. (Hancock had a horror of all forms of illness.) His enduring heroes were Buster Keaton, Laurel and Hardy, and Jacques Tati, all of whose comedy issued from a calm and logical centre, building by way of calamity and outrage, but never losing sight of the stillness of its core. He also revered Sid Field, whose routines he knew by heart, and to an even greater extent, W. C. Fields, who waged war on a sober world with a baroque verbal overkill ("I can lick my weight in wild flowers," he was once heard to boast) and whose way of dealing with a pesky blind man in one film was to steer him towards the highway, murderous with traffic. Hancock never dared to go to such extremes, but he often told of a pantomime in which he played a character called Jolly Jenkins whose chore at one stage in the proceedings was to coax an audience of children to join him in singing a ditty entitled "Every little piggy had a curly tail". It was not a success. Hancock forgot the words. The audience remained mute. "We stared at each other across the footlights in mutual hatred," Hancock recalled.

He was not a great teller of jokes, but he responded to the quiddities of life itself like a Bisto kid suddenly scenting his favourite aroma. He loved the desperation implicit in the billing of a variety artist called Kardomah who promised by way of the theatre poster to "fill the stage with flags". It was, in fact, all that he did. Flags sprouted from his sleeves, his collar, his shirt front, his trouser legs until they overflowed into the orchestra pit. Invariably he ended the first half of the bill. The interval was wholly occupied in gathering up the bunting. It was a hard act to follow, said Hancock.

He also relished the experience of taking tea with a provincial mayor who insisted on parading up and down the mayoral parlour wearing the mayoral hat, heavy with braid and nodding with plumes. It was quite a performance, but the mayoress was not impressed. "He thinks he cuts a dash," she told Hancock. "But by heck, he does look a bloody fool when it rains!"

What Hancock enjoyed, what he found funny, was the capsizing of dignity, the ultimate madness of logic. He admired performers who could skate over or through every neatly applied layer of thrift or caution and win through to some slightly illicit goal. Con men, even when he was the person conned, excited his admiration because in some small way they were out to outwit the system. Once he emerged, considerably shaken, from the barber's shop of Simpson's in Piccadilly clutching an ivory hairbrush. He did not want it, he had never wanted it. He had merely asked for a haircut, but the barber had persuaded him to buy the brush for £12. It was a fantastic sales pitch, said Hancock, worth every penny of what he had numbly paid. He would also recall a backstage salesman who used to haunt the dressing rooms at the Adelphi Theatre when he was appearing there in a Jack Hylton revue. Whisky was, at that time, in short supply, but the salesman – a retired army major was how he used to describe himself – had two lines to offer. The standard item was Johnny Walker Black

Hancock eating out with his first wife, Cicely: food could be funny

Label, which he was prepared to hand over at the black market price of £5 a bottle. But for men of discernment, said the major, he had a special brand called Night Rider. Naturally, he had to charge a little more. But £8 was nothing for nectar such as this. Hancock sampled a dram and privately pronounced it vile. But he urged all self-professed connoisseurs to buy it in bulk because he saw it as a weapon in the war against drinking snobs. If they bought it because they were told it was special without trusting their taste buds, then they deserved to be bilked. As a drinking man he had no truck with pretentious palates.

He frequently saw food as a subject for comedy, although sometimes the joke was peculiar and private. In Paris, for example, he would occasionally organise lunch parties in expensive restaurants, ordering a different dish for every guest with the injunction that they should 'dash it around', everyone sampling everyone else's meal. But, invariably, he would lead the company to a back-street bistro for the sweet course. The detour was not in the cause of good eating but to observe a ritual, the point being that the only sweet on offer was something described on the restaurant slate as "Le Cake". "And that's exactly what it is!" Hancock would jubilantly point out. "Yellow English fruit cake. Mind you, you can always douse it in brandy."

The flavour was unimportant. What Hancock enjoyed was the incongruity of the occasion, a touch of Bournemouth-sur-le-Seine.

Not that he was a zealot for home cooking. One day we met for a drink in a pub near Billingsgate where the fish porters instantly recognised Hancock. After a brief conference one of them came up bearing a newspaper parcel. "Just a small tribute from the lads," he said, pressing it into Hancock's hand. He opened it fearfully and revealed two fine bloaters embossed with newsprint. That afternoon they accompanied him to a script conference at the BBC, on to a bar in the evening, and then into a cinema where he left them under the seat. He was not ungrateful, he explained later, but he was beginning to get funny looks when his neighbours caught the smell.

Hancock did not invent situation comedy, although he was one of its greatest exponents. What he brought to it that was unique, was the understanding that no situation was utterly self-contained. Regardless of the dictates of the script, in Hancock's mind the story began long before the opening titles and continued after the final credit had rolled. He had a novelist's sense of plot development, with character as the starting point. Events could not be conceived arbitrarily. People behaved as they were bound to behave. They were committed to their comic destinies and when they denied their true natures the comedy fell flat.

He was forever speculating on what *made* people the way they were. One of his favourite lunching places was a hotel in Kensington which boasted the most comprehensive wine list in London. Hancock fancied himself as a wine expert (a role in which he could, at times, become wearisome), but his joy in visiting the place was further compounded by its ancient *sommelier* whose nose, after decades of dedicated drinking, had attained a rare bilberry hue. He was never entirely sober, never quite falling-down drunk. His progress through a crowded dining-room was a miracle of daring and judgment. He navigated a course between tables, chairs, and carelessly strewn handbags with never a downward glance. When a diner pretended to deliberate over the vintages inscribed on the wine list before plumping tamely for the house claret the famous nose would twitch its contempt. And Hancock would watch raptly. A nose like that was a career in itself, he would say. More than that, it was a monument.

For years he planned to use the *sommelier* – or a character based upon him – in a film or TV show. He gave him an invented

background, a lifeline (none of which would have featured in the action). He even conceived a glorious end: death by drowning in a cask of Echézaux. ("The only wine which sounds like a sneeze," he would say.) But the idea never took positive shape. Possibly it was because Hancock's own attitude was ambiguous (as a declared foe of winesmanship he none the less contributed to its mythology). But a more likely explanation was that he felt the story still had several chapters to run. He did not want to anticipate the way it came out.

Much of Hancock's life was spent in watching and waiting for the perfect anecdote (preferably true) which he would stow away until its perspectives had somehow become rooted in his own experience. Then and only then would he bring it out, not just as a funny story but as an illustration of his own point of view; a peephole through which he saw the world. Not all of the stories were flattering. It was useful at times, he said, to be known as a bit of a bastard. He liked to tell of the day he finally tired of a long-time house guest who over the years had featured as his stooge, his dresser, and general factotum. He was allegedly an Italian count and undeniably a lush. For several weeks he had billeted himself in Hancock's home, uninvited but eager to be of service, a fact which he stressed by rising before anyone else, washing the dishes and preparing an unasked-for breakfast. By the time the rest of the household was stirring he was phenomenally cheerful, a condition which Hancock eventually and correctly ascribed to a massive intake of booze, consumed while the dew was still on the grass. "He wasn't choosy," said Hancock, with some admiration. "It was once round the shelves before 8 a.m." The filching had to stop, though, he decided. One morning at 9 a.m., by which time the factotum was awash with his assorted tots, Hancock briskly led him to the car where his bag was already stowed, drove him to the end of the lane and pushed him wordlessly into the London-bound coach. The memory which gave him most pleasure was that of the factotum, still unaware that he had been deported, beaming woozily through a side window while the conductor, appalled by the prospect of having to cosset a drunk for forty miles, mouthed his *envoi* behind him. Hancock prided himself on his ability to lip-read. "What he was saying," he claimed, "was 'Rotten sod!' And he was probably right."

He believed himself to be a realist, but the reality could be

16 adjusted to suit his mood. There was the day when my wife and I

bought a set of dining chairs. There were five of them and we needed them to sit on. But to Hancock, who had been sounding off that morning on bourgeois pretensions and the curse of gentility, their purchase meant something sinister.

"What do you *need* chairs for?" he enquired – a trifle moodily, I thought.

"The usual reason."

"But they're *dining* chairs."

"We eat meals."

There was a short pause during which Hancock brooded some more. Then came the attack. "I suppose it'll be a three-piece suite next."

"I doubt it."

". . . and the vicar for tea."

"Not at all."

". . . join the League of Empire Loyalists."

"Hardly."

". . . run with the pack."

"Rubbish."

". . . vote Conservative."

The chairs were second-hand and cost slightly over £8. But no matter: for Hancock the principle was the thing. The chairs remained the skeleton in my closet which he would rattle whenever he felt so inclined.

He was fond of animals, but his sense of humour faltered when he read a newspaper paragraph in which the writer likened him to a St Bernard who had lost his keg in a snowdrift. Nor was he much amused when someone remarked on the similarity between his own large quarter-to-three feet and the splayed paws of one of my basset hounds. He refused the offer of one as a pet. "Can you just see us trotting along together?" he demanded. "They'd be entering me for Crufts next."

He disliked satire. Lenny Bruce left him cold and he was deeply wounded by a comic strip in the magazine *Private Eye* in which he was caricatured as 'Tony Halfcock', the egotist who made use of his friends and then abandoned them in the quest for solitary stardom. He was so offended that, for a time, he contemplated issuing a writ. What dissuaded him was the certainty that any such action would result in banner headlines and he was appalled by the prospect of

the consequent publicity.

In fact, he regarded all publicity as a necessary evil and most interviews as exercises in polite evasion. He did not intend to deceive, merely to defend his privacy. For years he refused to have his home photographed. As he explained to Dee Remmington in the *Sunday Graphic*: "There must be somewhere you can be absolutely private. I don't feel my private life is anyone's concern and that is why I don't like it photographed."

In the same interview he also confided that his current reading

Hancock and Cicely: when the marriage worked

(the year was 1959) included *The Anvil of Civilization* by Leonard Cottrell; that his most treasured possession was leisure; that he preferred country life to living in town; and that his future plans centred on making himself "as international as possible".

Dee Remmington asked him: "Are you afraid the public will tire of you?" And Hancock replied: "I expect to live a reasonable time and I want what little talent I have to last out. The fatal thing would be to overwork it. I could work three times harder than I do."

If he was not a comedian, he added, he knew pretty well what he would like to be: "An archaeologist or geologist. A job where you can trace things back to their origins."

A trailer for fame

Hancock's own origins were an odd blend of the respectable and the racy. His parents, Jack and Lily Hancock, ran a hotel in Bournemouth, a seaside resort where the very rich co-existed with genteel survivors from an Edwardian heyday, their pensions dwindling as the century progressed. Jack was a semi-pro entertainer – elegant, recalled Hancock, in white tie and tails – and the hotel was much frequented by variety artists visiting the town.

In later years Hancock reviled the platitudes of the trade. "The show must go on" and "There's no business like show business" were his two least favourite axioms. But, more thoroughly than he knew, he was steeped in its traditions. What he admired about the stars who visited his parents' hotel – a distinguished company from the 1930's including Clapham and Dwyer, Stainless Stephen, and Elsie and Doris Waters – was, first of all, their professionalism and secondly their apparent raffishness. Their professionalism, he realised, was their safety net, an insurance against unscrupulous managements, missing props, the thousand and one hazards of the variety circuit. The raffishness he saw as a licence to be different; an excuse in his own case for unpunctuality, borrowing money and forgetting to return it, brusqueness verging on bloody-mindedness – a wholesale contradiction, in fact, of the professional code which made the performer's life bearable. He never succeeded in reconciling the two, although he signalled a wry understanding of his predicament on one of his last variety tours by billing himself "Mr Show Business. ... Born in a Trunk". It was the kind of sentimental oversell which he had parodied for years. Applying it to himself was Hancock's way of kicking his own backside. But, characteristically, it was also a sideswipe at his public. "Believe that guff about me," he was saying, "and you'll believe anything."

His mother, Lily, was a redoubtable lady who adored her son (his elder brother, Colin, was killed in World War II; his younger brother, Roger, is now a highly respected agent) but who was acutely aware of his failings. He was equally fond of her, and when she was staying 21 with him he would often take her to visit his friends. At midnight as the drinks continued to flow and Hancock remained deep in boozy conversation she would call for her coat and kid gloves. "If I put these on he'll move," she used to say. "It always worked with his father." Usually it would work with Hancock too.

His memory was unreliable. Learning his lines for a television show was agony, but he had an almost total recall of acts which he had seen as a child and he could never forget his own disastrous début as a professional comic. It was not the career his parents had envisaged for him, but after a spell at Bradfield College (where he learned to play an excellent game of cricket, good enough to earn him a place in the Hampshire Junior County side) he spent only a few arid weeks as a shop assistant, then as a Grade III Civil Servant, before deciding that the actor's life was for him. Stuffed to his adolescent gills with gleanings of other men's material and kitted out in two-tone shoes and a curly brimmed trilby hat, he launched himself on a round of smokers and stag parties as Anthony Hancock, the Confidential

Roger and Tony Hancock: growing up among the stars

Comic. His act, as he described it in retrospect, was filthy beyond belief and it received its quietus after one memorable occasion when he was invited to top the bill at a social held at a Catholic church hall. Warmed by the footlights he told jokes about commercial travellers and lustful landladies, about landgirls and sergeant majors, about bishops and actresses, by which time he realised that he was playing to an empty hall. The audience had walked out. The vicar who had urged him to perform paid him his fee of 12s 6d and shook his head. "Such a pity about you, Hancock," he sighed. "I knew your father well."

The year was 1940. Hancock was seventeen at the time and his father had died six years previously. Remembering the way his audience had melted away he burned the offending script and disposed of the hat and the shoes. From that day on his act was wholly free of smut. He was far from being a puritan, but as his reputation grew so did his determination to preserve it from any taint of sexual innuendo. During his subsequent partnership with Sid James (who shared quarters with him, according to the script, in the house in Railway Cuttings) he worried constantly that audiences might think they were homosexual husband and wife. Visiting Paris long before Britain's bookstalls were liberated he would stock up on the slim green volumes of erotica published by the Olympia Press, but after reading them he would consign them – carefully torn in half – to the wastepaper basket. "Pity about that one," he would say wistfully, "but what if the customs found it? I can just see the headlines. 'Hancock charged with possession of porn'."

The church-hall social cured him once and for all of reliance on the blue gag for an easy laugh, but he was still uncertain what his comic style should be. He admired an extraordinary monologuist named Reggie Purdell who recited little fables – there was one about deer coming to drink at a forest pool – to the accompaniment of 'descriptive' piano music, and when Purdell announced that he was about to retire Hancock bought his repertoire. When he tried it out he realised instantly that, for him, it was useless. The style was the man. And Hancock was several light years away from Reggie Purdell.

When he did at last find material which suited him he clung to it for years. A revue sketch called "The Crooner", which Alan Simpson and Ray Galton together with Frank Muir and Denis Norden

Hancock's crooner: a period piece

wrote in 1953 as a parody of the Johnny Ray phenomenon, remained one of Hancock's standbys for at least a decade, long outlasting the vogue at which it had poked fun. Its chief prop was a blue drape suit, a jigsaw of strips of material clamped to the lining with press-studs which were ripped off twice-nightly by the crooner's frenzied fans. For the act Hancock also wore a pair of shoes with crêpe soles as thick as hamburgers. Midway through a song he would break off and point to his suffering feet. "I don't know how they do an hour and a half at the Palladium," he would confide to the audience. "I've got toes like globe artichokes." He was also faithful to an item called "The Bells" which began with Hancock declaiming the famous recitation in high Henry Irving style only to be interrupted by the diminutive Johnny Vyvyan answering the summons ("The bells! The bells!") with the tinkle of a tiny hand-bell clasped between finger and thumb. The performance ended with Hancock circling the stage and baying for sanctuary. "Sanctuary! Give me sanctuary!" he would beg, fine acting spraying from every pore. Then, abruptly, he would straighten up. "Sanctuarymuch," he'd say, and exit briskly, stage left. When he was feeling especially exuberant he would essay an impersonation of Nat 'King' Cole, the singer with whom he shared the bill on several variety tours. It was not very good; nor, in terms of strict accuracy, were his impressions of Robert Newton as Long John Silver, Charles Laughton as the Hunchback of Notre Dame, or George Arliss – an actor famous in the 1930's for his film portrayals of historical greats such as Disraeli and the Iron Duke. It was doubtful whether many members of Hancock's audience had even heard of Arliss let alone seen him. Not that it mattered. It was Hancock's personal revue of time past (the view through the peephole once again). Furthermore he was indifferent to the vagaries of taste. In his book good material did not date. After a while it became vintage.

Eventually he was to become one of the most innovatory of TV performers. ("The biggest battle I ever won," he said, "was to do comedy in close-up.") But his confidence and his technique took years to develop. During the war he served with the RAF Regiment, a preliminary to joining Ralph Reader's RAF *Gang Show* where he worked with Graham Stark and Peter Sellers, with whom he shared responsibility for looking after the Show's wardrobe. It was the *Gang Show* which taught him his essential business – how to control an audience, how to project a comic persona (at that time undeveloped), and how to handle material which, although it was unsuitable, could be milked to the ultimate. In a post-war show called *Wings* Ralph Reader gave him a song to sing entitled "I'm a Hero to My Mum" in which Hancock appeared as an earth-bound airman, perpetually consigned to cookhouse fatigues. Its final line went: "I don't care tuppence 'cos I know darn well I'm a hero to my mum." A production photograph of the act showing a phenomenally lean Hancock clutching a broom and singing soulfully into the spotlight was a weapon which could always be used to silence him in arguments about artistic integrity in later years. I once had a number of prints made and produced them, one at a time, when the debate became heated. Hancock did not relish being reminded of his apprentice years.

After being demobilised he drummed his head against the usual number of closed doors and, he claimed, almost starved in the winter of 1947, beating the cold only by staying resolutely in bed and eating quantities of a substance he described as "heavy sausage", washed down and given extra bulk by draughts of water. London was full of unemployed comics and Hancock's immediate circle included Eric Sykes, Michael Bentine, Spike Milligan, Robert Moreton, and an ex-Commando named Larry Stevens who wrote material both for Hancock and for the early *Goon Shows*, and who died tragically early.

In 1948 Hancock formed a double act with Derek Scott, a fine musician and pianist, whose poise concealed not only a deadpan sense of humour but also a capacity for hard bargaining. Together they auditioned for Vivian Van Damm, the owner of the Windmill Theatre, then reputedly the nude Mecca of the British Isles. There was scant competition for the title, but in the 1940's there seemed to be something unbelievably exotic (although far from erotic) in the spectacle of unclad ladies striking statuesque poses in which they remained motionless by order of the Lord Chamberlain, until the end-of-tableaux blackout. Between wads of naked flesh were sandwiched comics, conditioned – so it was said – to 'die with a smile'. While they were on stage they were virtually ignored by the predominantly male audience whose collective mind was fixed on more pneumatic things. Hancock and Scott were hired, although the negotiations briefly faltered when Hancock found himself quite incapable of referring to the great Van Damm as 'VD' – the soubriquet he favoured.

26   They were paid £30 a week – not a princely sum for six shows

With Peter Brough and Archie Andrews: never trust a wooden dummy

a day – but in 1948 the punishment had an even keener edge. The Olympic Games were being held in London and peering through the glare of the footlights Hancock became convinced that their mute reception was due to the fact that the audience waiting impatiently for the girls to return was largely composed of Mongolian discus-throwers who understood not a word of what was being said. To re-assure themselves that they were still in the land of the free they also did a stint at the Nuffield Centre, a luxury Forces canteen near Charing Cross Station, where free variety shows were staged for servicemen. BBC producers visited the place on talent-spotting safaris and, not for the first time, Hancock was noted as a comedian of promise.

Only eight years later in the first flush of his television fame Hancock's beginnings were curiously overlooked. It was as though recognition in the literal sense began when he took up residence at Railway Cuttings. The public saw what they liked and liked what they saw. But, in fact, Hancock's television fame was preceded by years of successful radio. From the Windmill he went into *Worker's*

Playtime, *Variety Bandbox* (on which he performed execrably due to a fit of nerves), *Educating Archie* (in which he was featured as tutor to the ventriloquist Peter Brough's dummy), and *All Star Bill* which went through several transformations before settling down as *Hancock's Half Hour*. Hancock was a veteran before he became a star.

The experience, especially that in *Educating Archie*, left its mark. For the first time he was saddled with a catchphrase: "Flipping kids". He was also given a constant but developing role, one which borrowed heavily from the famous feud manufactured between W. C. Fields and Charlie McCarthy, the dummy sired, or rather hewn, by the American ventriloquist Edgar Bergen. Brough's Archie Andrews was never given the obnoxious edge of Charlie McCarthy. But Hancock's detestation of the dummy (concealed during the run of the show) was unfeigned. Privately he would recite an anthology of Fields'

Hattie Jacques: superb comic support on the air and on the screen

McCarthy-directed abuse. "Get away from me before I cut you down into a venetian blind;" "Take him away before I squeeze every bit of wood alcohol out of his body;" "Someone must have left the kid out in the rain. His brain is warped." And, always superstitious, he confessed to the eerie suspicion that the dummy had a life of its own.

Years later when Hancock and I collaborated on the film *The Punch and Judy Man*, Hancock approached the name part with considerable misgiving. An elderly Punch and Judy operator named Joe Hastings was hired to manipulate the figure of Punch, but Hancock decided that he too should have a working knowledge of how to operate the puppets and – more importantly – how to speak with Punch's voice. This is achieved by the use of a swozzle – a small tin disc like a kazoo – which is concealed in the mouth and gives speech an odd

Hancock in revue at the Adelphi with Joan Turner and Jimmy Edwards

metallic resonance. From the start, Hancock developed a morbid fear of swallowing his swozzle (a fairly common occurrence among amateurs, Joe Hastings rashly warned him). But, more seriously, he became convinced that the figure of Punch himself was a malign presence and not one which could be dispelled by cheerful abuse. It was a premonition he felt doubly justified when Hastings died of cancer shortly after the film was completed.

During his early flowering on radio, however, there were no demons to be kept at bay. He also scored brilliantly in the stage shows *London Laughs* and *Talk of the Town* with Jimmy Edwards in 1952 and 1954, but his loathing of long runs led to brisk sparring with the impresario, Jack Hylton, a tough Lancashire-born ex-bandleader, who was more than a match for Hancock's schemes to slip the bonds of his contract. When *Talk of the Town* was playing in Blackpool (the intention being to transfer it to London at the end of the summer season) Hancock produced a medical certificate signed by a psychiatrist who testified that if his patient continued in the show his health would be seriously affected.

Hylton was unimpressed. The psychiatrist's certificate bore an address in Bolton – Hylton's own home town – and the local lad made plain to Hancock that no provincial opinion was weighty enough to break the contract. Hancock never forgave Hylton for his intransigence. And as Tony's brother Roger Hancock recalls, Hylton's own rancour remained just as keen. While working as stage manager in one of Hylton's later shows Roger was summoned to the master's presence to explain why various cues for lights and music had been mismanaged. He did his best to spell out a reason until he became aware that Hylton was studying him with a sharp and suspicious eye.

"What's your name?" he demanded.

"Hancock," Roger admitted.

The impresario slumped in his chair. "Jesus Christ," he murmured, staring heavenwards. "Don't send me another one."

Educating Archie was written by Eric Sykes, a brilliantly gangling Tati-like performer in his own right, but whose versatility – the skill with which he could tailor his comedy to a diversity of styles – was not the key which eventually released Hancock's greatest potential. He was also the author of Hancock's first TV shows, which were only moderately successful. But Hancock needed a writer – or writers – who could sense what was intrinsically funny in the man and provide the ambience, the situation in which he could be a comic and only slightly exaggerated approximation of himself. He found them in October 1951 when he met Alan Simpson and Ray Galton, two exceedingly raw recruits to the business of comedy writing who had first met when they were both patients in a TB sanatorium and whose first scripts were broadcast over the hospital radio.

It was always an edgy relationship. Hancock was secretly in awe of Galton and Simpson's acute sense of what was risible about his pretensions (his winemanship for example), his hunger for education (encyclopaedias and potted histories of the world formed the basis of his reading), and his not-always-simulated grand manner. In patent self-defence he referred to them as "the boys", a phrase which, on the face of it, was affectionate – and there was, indeed genuine affection between them – but which also established the pecking order in their social and professional dealings. Galton and Simpson countered – consciously or otherwise – by acting as ostentatiously plain men. Wine which Hancock would offer to the company as something for connoisseurs they would sip and dismiss as "Good plonk". They would also, on occasion, scoff at Hancock's plans to find for himself an attic in Paris (for years he would talk with an almost adolescent yearning for a Left-Bank hideaway). And their wholly bogus insularity would drive Hancock to a fine frenzy.

What mattered, though, was the fruit of their collaboration, the radio shows which became the television series and which revolutionised British comedy in the 1950's. What they dispensed with was plot. Not immediately; but throughout 160 scripts for both radio and television the storylines became slimmer and the brew of character thickened. Hancock himself – the belligerent but vulnerable yearner; whose drenching disappointments were resolutely shrugged off like dew from a gabardine; who, far from being the classic figure of the clown (that is, he who gets slapped) was the first to slap back – was the rock that Galton and Simpson tossed into life. The ripples that came back, then the waves that mounted as Hancock struck for the shore was the humour they created. It was not the invention of situation comedy, but it did without doubt score a new high-water mark.

Hancock's Half Hour came to BBC television in 1956 and established new
ratings records. Success derived from the scripts by Ray Galton and Alan Simp-

son, productions by Duncan Wood, the playing of regulars including Joan Heal, Arthur Mullard and Mario Fabrizi, and Hancock's own innovatory timing

Jail in Railway Cuttings

Collaborations are always mysterious affairs. Their constitution defies analysis. The most successful mergers show no joins (Frank Muir and Denis Norden; Billy Wilder and I. A. L. Diamond). Each partner, whatever the number, has a role to play. But the blend, the homogeneity, should be total. For a while Hancock implied that he did, in fact, write many of his own lines. He relished being considered a writer. But his true contribution was himself, his personality, his physical presence. In any situation, real or invented, Hancock acted as catalyst. The world, viewed through his eyes, underwent a subtle change. Perspectives altered. In rapid succession, according to his mood, he could be con man or victim; exploiter or exploited, realist or dreamer.

The repertory company of supporting players – most of whom achieved stardom, and as soon as they did were dropped from the Hancock roster – provided a setting for a hero as fully fleshed as he was unlikely. There's no doubt that Hancock was loved. But the character he projected was far from lovable. He was vain, he was pompous, he was a bully. But the neuroses, the grumbles, the psychic warts which he displayed were common to three-quarters of the island race. He was truly representative and so he could be excused.

The founding members of the radio troupe included Kenneth Williams, Hattie Jacques, Sid James, and Bill Kerr, and rarely has a company been so shrewdly chosen. Hancock, of course, was the centre-piece – the squire of 23 Railway Cuttings, East Cheam; a would-be actor kitted out for the part in derelict Homburg and ankle-length black overcoat in whose astrakhan collar generations of moths had lived and died. Sid James was the crooked friend; an investor in goods which had mysteriously fallen off the backs of lorries, instigator of get-rich-quick schemes which invariably failed. Bill Kerr was the colonial cousin from down-under, a remittance man in reverse. Hattie Jacques was Miss Pugh, an under-employed secretary, whose appetite, complained Hancock, kept him in penury. And Kenneth Williams was everyone else – policeman, vicar, test-pilot – whose

With Bill Kerr and Kenneth Williams, soon to be dropped from the roster

scripts usually included the directions 'Snide voice here', a requirement which he could meet with infinite variations. It was here that Williams first coined his catchphrase 'Stop messin' about' – a piece of comic shorthand of which Hancock ultimately disapproved.

The less that actually happened in the scripts, the more Hancock liked them. There were delirious moments such as a duel between Hancock and Miss Pugh as to the rightness of buying forty-three packets of cornflakes so that Hancock can complete his set of giveaway plastic guardsmen. ("Dear Sir," he writes to the manufacturer, "I hereby warn you that if you discontinue putting guardsmen in my cornflakes before I've got the set, I shall in future eat porridge. Yours sincerely, A. Hancock. Age seven-and-a-half." Long pause. "There," he adds. "That'll frighten them.") There was also the surrealist programme when Hancock, installed in the cockpit of a test plane, hears a rapping on the roof and discovers Kenneth Williams hitching a stratospheric ride on the canopy. But his favourite show – and that of millions of listeners – was the one in which the boredom of one

Sunday afternoon was anatomised with a thoroughness and loathing in which long silences and *non sequiturs* distilled the desperation of the suburbs. The silences were increasingly important to Hancock, who knew to an uncanny degree how long a punch line could be delayed or how pregnant a pause could be allowed to become before the longed-for delivery. He distrusted clichés, but he improved and extended the one which stipulates: "Make 'em laugh. Make 'em cry. But, above all, make 'em wait."

He was also a collector of non-events. In the Sunday afternoon show, as the day draws on, Hancock seeks inspiration in the wallpaper. It's a God-awful design, but perhaps he can find pictures there. "There's an old man with a pipe," he suggests desperately. "Screw your eyes up. Stare hard. Concentrate on that bit by the serving hatch." It was pure Hancock. The elevation of trivia to ward off *ennui* was, he insisted, an enduring strain in the English character. He found most of his prize items in a regular column of news-briefs in the London *Evening News*. "Rats build nest in mayor's top-hat," he announced one day. "Mother of twins exhibits collection of lemonade bottles." He was convinced that an entire programme could be built up from similar gems, all genuine, all tiny monuments to desperation.

Another notion, also unfulfilled, was to construct a sketch in which all the characters were named after English villages. "Bovey Tracey" was one of his favourites, and his delight when he was once staying with me in Kent in finding a signpost pointing to "Throwley Forstall" was intense. "Small-part actor," he decided. "Walks through French windows saying, 'Tennis, anyone?'" Hancock's ideas were fresh, funny and unremitting. But he forgot them as quickly as they came to mind. What he needed was a Boswell to keep him constant company.

On radio, *Hancock's Half Hour* was a slow starter. The BBC Audience Research Report for the show broadcast on 2nd November 1954 revealed that only 12 per cent of the adult population of the UK heard the programme, but suggested that while there was an unenthusiastic response to the show as a whole (an appreciation index figure of 52) there was no doubt that Hancock himself enjoyed widespread popularity. By the end of the second series public enthusiasm had multiplied beyond all expectations (except those of Hancock) and in 1956 the *Half Hour* made the move to BBC television.

Not for the first time Hancock went in for a little house-cleaning.

Hancock with Arthur Askey, the hardiest of comic perennials

Bill Kerr was dropped from the show. Kenneth Williams went after six weeks. Hattie Jacques put in the occasional appearance. But, for the time being, the duo of Hancock and Sid James remained firm. Much has been said on the subject of Hancock's alleged disloyalty to old colleagues, but the reasons for his acts of real and abrupt ruthlessness – which were usually construed as professional jealousy – were quite different. He had the temperament, the ego of a great star. He was a perfectionist and a born worrier. Anything – or anyone – which stood between him and some so-far-unimagined goal had to be removed. He did not grudge his colleagues their success. He was,

Hancock on screen:
"Make 'em laugh.
Make 'em cry.
Make 'em wait."

in fact, uncommonly generous with funny lines which, as the star of the show, he could have cannibalised. But he was tormented by his own potential. He disliked and feared the idea that successful comedy depended on creating a formula which, while it fed him, also held him in thrall. The marvellously baroque vocabulary created for him by Galton and Simpson began to grow irksome. The flights of rhetoric – in *The Blood Donor*, for example – in which he could speculate about his pedigree were thoroughly acceptable. Told that he belongs to a rare blood group he positively glows. "Rare, eh? Of course I'm not surprised. I've always felt instinctively that I was somehow distinctive from the rest of the herd, you know. Something apart. I never fitted into society. That explains it. One of nature's aristocrats." But the verbal prat-falls, the return to the *patois* of Railway Cuttings where Hancock was expected to refer to a nose as a "hooter", where to be eccentric was to be "bonkers", and where "Stone me!" was his traditional expletive became, in his eyes, barnacles on the hull of a craft which he wanted to streamline more and more.

The public, however, loved the formula as it was. The radio show continued with undiminished success and in 1957 the televised *Half Hour* was reaching 23 per cent of the adult population of the UK, earning for Hancock the title of Comedian of the Year from the Guild of Television Producers and Directors. Typically, Hancock shrugged off the honour by keeping the award – a bronze mask – in the downstairs lavatory of his house at Lingfield in Surrey. But – also typically – he was quite aware that it was a port of call which most visitors to the house would make at some time or another. By November 1959 the show was reaching an audience of 27 per cent and by May 1961 it had climbed to a massive 30 per cent.

Meanwhile, there had been many changes in the style of production. Traditionally television comedy was either transmitted live or on tape that was impossible to edit. But the imperfections inherent in the method were intolerable to Hancock. No doubt improvements would have come about gradually. But the incident of the shaking house – a bijou residence at the end of the main runway at London Airport which, according to the script, Hancock and Sid James were trying to sell – accelerated the progress. It was no coincidence that Hancock's brother, Roger, did – and, in fact, still does – live in a house near Heathrow. Describing a fraternal visit Hancock would invariably mime the family at dinner, claiming that between the soup and the savoury, if a plane was to take off nearby all hands would seize the table, plates, and cutlery to save them from being swept away in the slipstream. It was a pardonable exaggeration and it provided the basis for an excellent comedy situation.

The set for the programme was flimsily built. The climax to the sketch was that the house should fall apart, but disintegration set in early when Hancock placed his hand on a table in the middle of the room and felt it quake. For the rest of the show he was forced to remain rooted to the spot, bracing the scenery, making nonsense of carefully planned camera angles, confusing the rest of the cast, and trying to suppress his own mounting hysteria. At the appropriate moment he released the table, which collapsed along with the rest of the house of TV cards.

Crisis had been averted, but Hancock was determined that it should never happen again. He and the producer, Duncan Wood – a great man in any emergency – devised a system whereby the 30-

Writers Ray Galton and Alan Simpson: watching the man, seeing the comedy 41

Hancock's most
famous TV programme,
The Blood Donor
with June Whitfield
and Frank Thornton

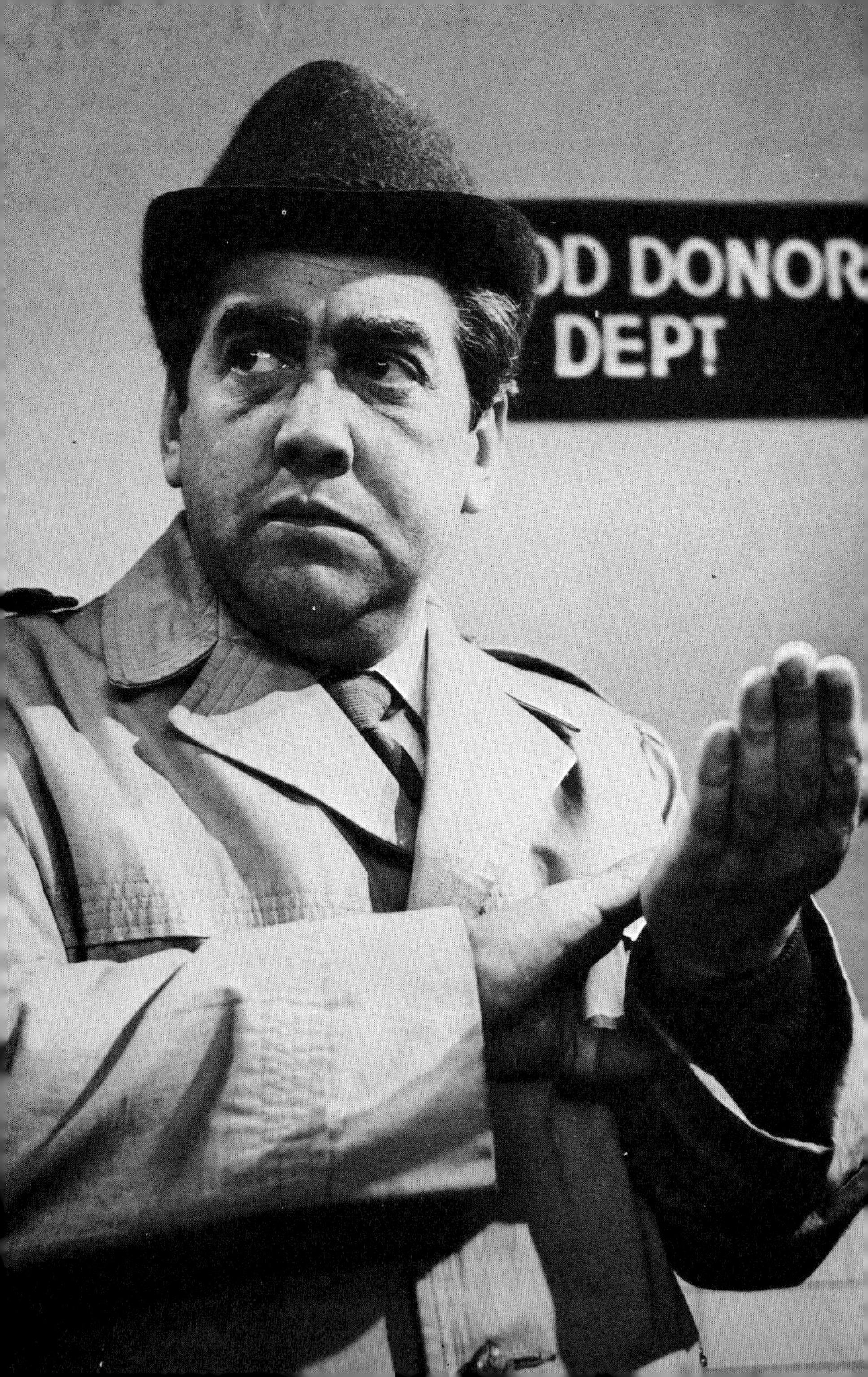
OD DONOR
DEPT

minute show was divided into several scenes between which the recording could be stopped, the cameras moved, dialogue checked, and lights re-positioned. It was a simplified version of what was already standard practice in film studios, but in television terms it was costly and unprecedented. Hancock over-rode all objections by refusing to sign up for another TV series unless his and Wood's method was adopted. It was one occasion when star-power was used to the advantage of all concerned.

Stardom, however, was a growing worry to Hancock. He sought it, but he also feared it. And accordingly he tried to tame the myth by debunking it. I first met Hancock when I was asked to interview him for a literary magazine (a sure sign of his growing status). He and first wife Cicely were then sharing a flat in London with two enormous poodles named Charlie and Mr Brown. Charlie was a happy extrovert, but Mr Brown was a nervous wreck. Hancock said that he saw ghosts. They lived in what might charitably be described as comfortable squalor. The beds were rarely made. The kitchen – although Cicely was an excellent cook – was a breeding ground for botulism. And the floor of the lavatory was paved with layer upon layer of letters – fan mail which Hancock had somehow never got round to answering.

After much deliberation Hancock decided to move to the country and bought the house at Lingfield. Its name was Val Fleuris, but Hancock instantly re-christened it MacConkey's – the name of the previous owner – which he also adopted as the name of his own short-lived film production company. There were cows in the surrounding meadows, strings of race-horses filing past to their stable along the road, and – as Hancock became nervously aware – a succession of mysterious bumps in the night.

I lived only a few miles away and Hancock insisted that I should experience the phenomenon for myself. Together we sat in an upstairs room, a bottle of brandy between us, and waited until – at nightfall – the ceiling above us reverberated as though a tennis ball were being bounced from end to end of the attic. We investigated, but found nothing. Hancock summoned the rodent exterminator, who put down poison. For a while the bumps continued and then ceased. We inspected the attic by flashlight and found two dead squirrels. Tears poured down Hancock's face. "Poor little sods," he said and gave them to the gardener to bury.

His approach to animals was unashamedly anthropomorphic. For him they had humanised personalities; their behaviour could only be assessed in human terms. His favourite light reading was the Christopher Robin books by A. A. Milne. He and Cicely (whom he nicknamed 'Wol' after the wise old owl in one tale) read them to each other in bed at night. Their joint favourite was the saga of Tigger who knew what he liked. But Hancock's idea of the perfect tragic hero was the donkey, Eeyore, forever being robbed of his thistles. He thought of himself as Pooh Bear, rotund and put-upon, the composer of little hums – an accomplishment of which Hancock, whose musical shortcomings were pronounced, was deeply envious.

His musical taste was, in fact, quite random. Cicely was a more than proficient pianist (especially of Chopin), but Hancock did not encourage her to play. The piano was kept in a room papered in Wedgwood blue with white woodwork and Hancock found its gentility overwhelming. His own instrument was the record player and his selection of albums ranged from Rimsky-Korsakov to male voice choirs, each of which he pronounced during a fit of enthusiasm as the only music worth hearing. During an evening's listening he would single out one record which he would play time and time again, blandly ignoring the protests of other listeners whose tastes were more catholic. Once at a party at my house he heard an album by the singer Carmen MacRae and instantly fell in love with it. I tried to buy another copy, but finding that it had been deleted from the catalogue gave him my own and for months he played nothing else. One track in particular, "Midnight Sun", enraptured him. It sounds excessive, but there is no other word for his brand of enthusiasm. "Listen to the bitch," he would say fondly as the singer's voice wound sinuously about the Lionel Hampton tune. "Just listen to what she gets away with." Judy Garland sparked an even fiercer passion. He was responding, he knew, to the melodrama of the performance – the flutter in the voice, the catch in the heart, the threat of imminent collapse. But, also, he warmed to the artistry which walked a knife edge. Like recognised like. He was contemptuous of her homosexual following. "She doesn't need that lot," he used to declare. And then he would recant. "But she needs somebody," he would say. "We all do."

At the same time he resented the growing public assumption that his success was really that of a business agglomerate: Hancock and Co. It was not that he was jealous of the success of his associates or

Hancock and Cicely on *Shemara*, a barge that was briefly their home

that he wanted to deny them their proper due. But – whatever the contribution of Galton and Simpson, however unstinting the support of Sid James – Hancock saw himself, essentially, as a solo performer, whose act was fed, if not by stooges, then by lesser lights. He preached equality, but he was no democrat. If it had been possible he would have liked to have written the script, performed all parts, and conducted the orchestra. In his own mind he probably did. What he was seeking was the kind of perfection which exists only in the imagination. His restlessness was, in effect, a series of forays – many of them leading up blind and bitter alleys – where he sought the impossible.

For others, though, it created bewilderment and pain. At Hancock's insistence comic regulars in the *Half Hour* were replaced by guest actors (Raymond Huntley, Jack Hawkins, André Morell) all of whom, said Hancock, gave the sketches a greater dimension of reality. At the same time he developed a passionate loathing of 23 Railway Cuttings, the address where he had found fame, but which – like any local lad whose career was on the upgrade – he felt he had outgrown.

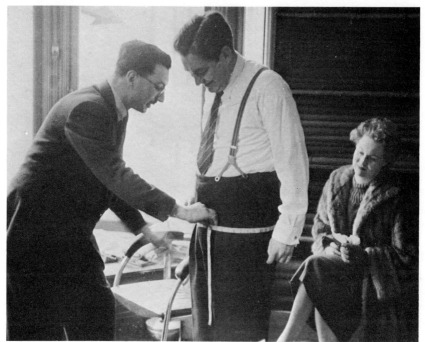

Hancock shunned tailors. He and fashion ignored each other

The problem was: where to turn next. Perhaps, he mused, his future lay in straight acting? He appeared in a Galton and Simpson adaptation of Gogol's *The Inspector General* and was funny, touching, and original in a part already identified with Danny Kaye. He played the lead in a TV adaptation of H. G. Wells's *The Man Who Could Work Miracles*. The reception was gratifying, but Hancock was unconvinced. He had great difficulty in learning his lines, a problem which was at one time made worse by an African grey parrot which he kept on a perch at one end of the bar at MacConkey's.

Hancock's learning method was to record all the parts of the other actors in the show, leaving appropriate gaps for his own lines. He would then play the tape back with his cues ready and waiting. Unfortunately, the parrot was what was known in the business as 'a fast study', and would chip in with irrelevant dialogue which threw Hancock completely off his stroke. The parrot was disposed of. But Hancock's irresolution remained. In some respects he was utterly realistic. The idea of a long stage run appalled him, not because he feared being less than word perfect (although he was incapable of ad-libbing and

Hancock quit driving after an accident, still bought costly cars

for his later TV shows depended largely on cue boards) but because he knew that he would never be able to sustain the self-discipline of repeating the same part night after night. He was too easily bored.

In 1959 he was again voted Comedian of the Year by the Guild of Television Producers and Directors, while Galton and Simpson took the award as Writers of the Year. He completed his television series in November with a record viewing figure of thirteen-and-a-half million viewers. But the next series of ten, which he completed recording in May 1960, was the last time he was ever to work with Sid James.

The friendship with Sid and his wife Valerie was maintained, at least on the surface. But Hancock – while convinced that he was doing the right thing in making a clean professional break – was nagged incessantly by guilt, and to see old friends from whom he had parted simply reminded him of what others felt (and said) to be desertion. Ironically, though, he struck up a new friendship with John Freeman, a former editor of the *New Statesman*, Labour politician, and diplomat-to-be, who interviewed him on the BBC TV series *Face to Face*. It was a thorough but far from ruthless grilling, but in the course of the 30-minute conversation Hancock revealed that he did not want

Grilled by John Freeman on *Face to Face*, Hancock admired his inquisitor

to father any children, that he was an agnostic, and that his earnings – although he refused to be more specific – were in the region of £30,000 a year.

He was, in fact, abnormally secretive about money and, while far from being mean, loathed the physical act of parting from anything he had earned. He was in the habit of running up quite sizeable bills at local pubs because he rarely carried cash on his person ("Like the Queen," I told him once, to his marked non-amusement). One day when a car salesman called to deliver a new Mercedes which he had ordered he signed a cheque for £5,000 and then instantly downed a tumbler of neat brandy to help repair the shock. He lived in fear of penury. When he first visited America, as an act of homage he went to see Stan Laurel, the veteran comedian whose classic films with Oliver Hardy were regularly shown on American TV. "And he doesn't get a penny for any of the repeats," reported Hancock in tones of pure outrage. "There he is, the poor bugger; another genius who got screwed."

He was a generous host, but at some moment which no one could predict the brake would be applied to his munificence, sometimes with ludicrous results. In the summer of 1960 he made his first major feature film, *The Rebel*, scripted by Galton and Simpson, and after the press show we spent the afternoon analysing the picture over drinks which grew larger and larger, winding up with a suite at the Ritz where an ebullient Hancock ordered a fine vintage port to help digest the dinner. We awoke the next day with severe hangovers, but mine was lessened by the sight of Hancock, swathed in a bath-towel, like a surly Nero, tipping what was left of the port back into an empty vodka bottle and corking it with a paper napkin. "It's fantastic stuff," he explained. "If we leave it here the waiters will only nick it."

The Rebel, in which Hancock played a suburban clerk who becomes an action painter in Paris (his technique is to pour paint on to a canvas stretched on the floor and make bicycle tracks through the goo), was coolly received by most critics, but it was a pronounced financial success. Hancock, however, had no percentage of the profits – a fact which irked him from the start. Perhaps he was thinking of Stan Laurel watching the TV entrepreneurs grow rich on his old movies while, towards the end, he subsisted on handouts. Again he resolved that whatever films he made in the future he would not be short-changed in the same way.

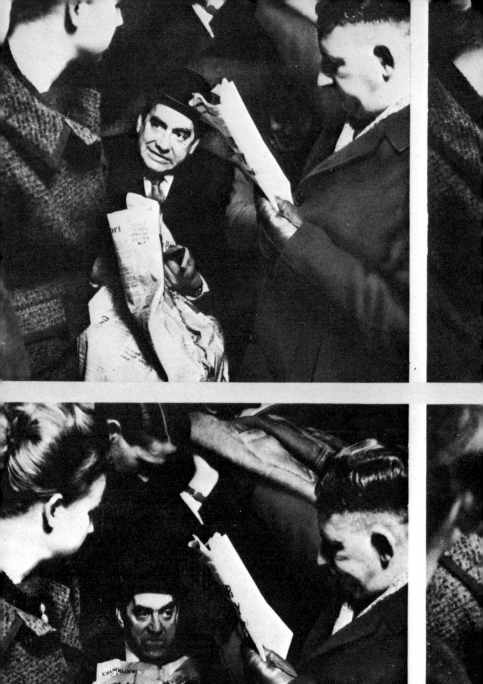

Frustration, rage,
despair:
high in Hancock's
repertoire

Hancock's favourite moment in *The Rebel*, a film he loathed

Action painting in *The Rebel*; critical knocks but profitable

One is one

In the spring of 1961 he toured the provinces, packing 3,000-seater cinemas with his old stage act, and returned to London to start work on what was to be his final series of *Hancock's Half Hour*. He was out of Railway Cuttings and the divorce from Sid James had been made absolute (at least, in Hancock's mind). His new television home was a seedy bed-sitter in Earl's Court, a cunningly constructed limbo in which Hancock – minus the Homburg and the coat with the astrakhan collar – could make a new life for himself. Not entirely, of course. Galton and Simpson's opening script – establishing the locale, the mood, and the promise – is a classic which gave Hancock superb material with which to extemporise. But no other actor could have done it justice. It is, quite simply, about a man alone with an infinity of an evening stretching ahead of him. How can he fill it? With intellectual press-ups perhaps. The equipment's there: *Das Kapital*, *The Decline of the West*, *The Outsider*. But Hancock's immediate problem is how to blow the perfect smoke ring, an exercise which singes his lip and sets him rummaging through the medicine chest for a remedy. He rejects the bottle labelled 'Master A. Hancock, Lower 4B' and settles for a dab of butter: "A touch of the old New Zealand". Studying his reflection in the mirror he prods his teeth and speculates: "Is that loose or is it me fingers going in and out? I wonder which one's the bicuspid. I've been wanting to know that for years. Bicuspid. It's a funny word, that is. Bi'cuspid. Bicus'pid. Bicuspid'. 'Bicuspid, he's a handsome devil, Sir George!' Ha ha ha! 'Have at you, sir. Have at you!' Bicuspid. I suppose it's Latin. Bi meaning two. One on each side. Cus, meaning to swear. Pid, meaning ... pid. Yes, Greek for teeth probably. That's it then. Bicuspid – two swearing teeth. I suppose so. I bet I'm not so far out anyway."

He sags back on the bed. "It's very hard to be an intellectual these days," he reflects. "Let's have a go at old Bertie Russell." Two sentences on he reaches for the dictionary. Then again, and again. "It's in English," he reassures himself. "I should know what he's talking about. He's a human being, same as me, using words, English words,

available to us all." Useless. He abandons Russell and tries a thriller. Seconds on he reaches for the dictionary once more.

The phone rings. The call is for Fred, the previous tenant. A girl is inviting him to a party. Hancock manages to manoeuvre himself into the position of substitute. He describes himself: "You know . . . sort of well built. No, no. Not fat. Well built, I said. Tallish. No, not quite six foot. Taller than average, though." And how will he know her? She'll be wearing leopardskin tights and a green sweater, she tells him. He's inflamed by the prospect. An Earl's Court swinger. How to meet the challenge? He chooses his outfit: jeans, an open-necked shirt with a medallion.

He prepares his toilet. No electric razor for him. "You can't beat the cold steel and the badger. All that electrical rubbish – little wheels spinning all over the place – that's for callow youths and peach fluff – not a man's beard." He slaps on after-shave lotion and instantly regrets it (the astringent scalds his jowls) followed by a heavy dusting of talc. "It'll drive her berserk," he muses. "Stops them dead in their tracks at twenty-five yards, this stuff."

But it's not to be. The girl in leopardskin tights telephones to say that Fred has turned up. Hancock is left on his own. "Stupid women!" he complains. "Why do they phone in the first place? Why don't they leave you alone? Leopardskin tights at her age. How revolting. She sounds a right crone. That was a lucky escape, I nearly got sucked into a social whirlpool there . . . diverted from my lofty ideals into a life of debauchery. The fleshpots of West London have been cheated of another victim. Eve has proffered the apple and Adam has slung it right back at her."

But how can he occupy the wasteland of the evening? He tries television, opting for a Western rather than culture with Professor Bronowski. No contact there he decides: "He's all right on theories, but when it comes to adding up sums he's right out of his depth." The picture, when he turns on the set, is on the blink. He experiments patiently, trailing the aerial about the room, sitting on the window sill, and viewing through the pane. The announcer comes on to apologise for interference due to circumstances beyond their control. Hancock returns to Bertrand Russell and then surrenders. "No," he decides. "I'll read it tomorrow."

What's revealing is to see how closely Galton and Simpson had modelled the television Hancock on the real man. His fascination with words, for example, was not invented. He relished odd and genuine sounds. "Funicular", for example, and "parsimonious". Watching a children's quiz he was torn between concern for the young contestant and hilarity at her understandable error when – asked the name of the posts used to rope a ship to the quay-side – she replied "Bollocks". His preoccupation with shaving was also genuine; so was his total inability to cope with anything mechanical. Once, I remember him fuming because an electric razor (the type which did indeed have "little wheels spinning all over the place") would not work. I opened it up and three months' accumulation of compressed hair sprang across the room. It had not occurred to Hancock that the razor needed cleaning since the day he bought it. The Bertrand Russell joke also bore close to home. The walls of Hancock's office were lined with volumes of popular philosophy, but they were more handled than read, as though Hancock believed that the ideas they contained could be transmitted by osmosis rather than by actual study.

More obliquely, Galton and Simpson had also hinted at the nature of at least some of Hancock's dealings with women. He regarded them, with few exceptions, as a Second Sex to be enjoyed and indulged; but also, if need be, to be exploited and abandoned. Women, in general, saw only Hancock's endearing side – the bafflement, the teddy-bear appeal, the unvoiced but implicit invitation to improve him. He made capital of his helplessness. But he had pockets of self-sufficiency which he could unzip with bewildering speed and ruthlessness. Once, when we were closeted in a service flat working on a script, a woman friend of Hancock's answered all his telephone biddings to bring office equipment, food, and drink with good humour and alacrity. One evening, however, they quarrelled – as they had done before – and the woman, who had previously threatened suicide, locked herself in the bathroom where (I recalled with sudden horror) Hancock had left a stock of razor blades. What if she used one to slash her wrists? I asked him. Hancock poured himself a large drink. "Let's hope she does a good job," he replied.

Galton and Simpson, I think, scored brilliant variations on the failings which Hancock himself acknowledged: his petulance, his flirtations with the establishment (debating with clerics rivalled cricket as Hancock's favourite sport), his vacillation towards the political Left which was never consolidated – although Michael Foot remained one of his greatest heroes. But, just as importantly, they

Getting to grips with words. Hancock alone in his TV bedsitter

hinted at his idealism – unactivated because of sloth and circumstance, but a genuine impulse all the same. Hancock refused to sign petitions or ally himself to any particular cause, however worthwhile he believed it to be. But he was fearful of being exploited; fearful, too, of being thought fashionable. He could never believe that any motive was entirely pure. Somewhere among the ideals – however they dazzled – lurked a few grains of self-interest. He wanted the world to be a better place. He wanted himself to be a better man. But how to achieve it? That was the question. He philosophised, pondered, and, towards the end, became desperate. But, always, he tried to distinguish between the good wheat and the easy chaff.

Hancock's would-be-heroic side was given a superb airing in Galton and Simpson's *Mayday* episode in which Hancock, the radio ham, has installed a massive bank of short-wave equipment in his bed-sitter. Twiddling the knobs he soliloquises: "Ah, it's marvellous to be able to converse with people all over the world. People different to yourself, with something new to say; it broadens your outlook, increases your knowledge of things. I bet there's not many people round here who know it's not raining in Tokyo. I suppose I must lead what the social workers call a full life. The world is my oyster, I can dip in and have a basinful of anywhere I fancy. Ooh, these headphones don't half make your ears hot!" He removes the earphones, like great padded basins. "Dear, oh dear, like two braised lamb chops under there, they are."

The chat continues. He promises his Malayan correspondent a tray of bread pudding, then inspects his milk bottle. "Hallo, the blue tits have been at the top of the milk again. Look at my gold top, pecked to ribbons it is. They must have beaks like pneumatic drills, some of them. I will *not* have great feathered heads stuck in my milk bottles, guzzling the cream."

Eventually he picks up a Mayday distress signal. Somewhere in the Atlantic, three hundred miles off the African coast, the motor yacht *Billet Doux* is drifting out of control and sinking fast. Hancock tries to take down its exact position. His pencil breaks. The Mayday signal fades and gives way to a soap opera, then to Victor Sylvester dance music. A Japanese voice cuts in to inform the world that it is not raining in Tokyo. "Will you get off the air, you Oriental fool!" explodes Hancock. A neighbour, whose wife complains of the noise, half demolishes the set. Repairing it, Hancock whirls dials until –

without warning – the light goes off. He puts a shilling in the meter and, amazingly, re-establishes contact. The yacht is sinking fast. Hancock scribbles down its position. He's to be a hero after all. And then, one by one, the valves of his set explode.

Hours later he's informed that the weather-conscious ham in Tokyo has caught the Mayday signal and that all's well. That evening, clamped in his headphones, he receives another distress call from the Indian Ocean. Again the boat is going down fast, but this time Hancock knows what to do. "I'm not very good at this sort of thing," he tells the sinking mariner. "You'd be much better off with someone else." He turns the dial for Malaya. "The sun's shining," he reports. "There's a bit of cloud about, but it's not raining. And your bread pudding's in the post."

The series – which included *The Blood Donor* – reached an average viewing figure of fifteen-and-a-half million people. Hancock had never been more deservedly popular; nor had his bargaining position ever been stronger. What he yearned for was an international reputation. And he was convinced that he could win it through films. But the problem, as he saw it, was to find the proper subject – a story which would give him as much scope as Jacques Tati or Chaplin – and it was here that he fell out with Galton and Simpson.

They wanted an international success just as ardently as he did and over the next six months, without being paid, they worked on three scripts, each tailor-made for Hancock. The first cast him as the black sheep of four brothers who returns from abroad to disrupt their placid and successful lives. The second sent him on a world cruise: a plotless but incident-packed excursion. The third (tentatively entitled *The Day Off*) was about the use and mis-use of leisure. Hancock rejected them all after either a cursory reading or an angry discussion.

Finally he announced that he no longer wanted them to write for him at all. No more films. No more television. The BBC pleaded with him to change his mind, but he was adamant. At the same time he dismissed his agent, Beryl Vertue, and insisted that his brother, Roger, should leave London Management – the firm which had represented him – and act solely on his behalf. It was a great burning of bridges, and while the smoke was still thick over the land he telephoned me with a proposition. "How would you like to write a film with me?" he asked.

"Mayday! Mayday!" Hancock to the rescue as the Radio Ham

Letting it all out

On the face of it I was an odd choice for the role of Hancock's script-writer. On the credit side I was passionately interested in films (for several years I'd been a film critic). I was fairly experienced in writing for television. My first novel, a social comedy, was about to be published. But I had not yet been blooded in the ways of working with Hancock or anyone remotely like him. The invitation, though, was too good to resist. And as we discussed it one wet September day, just as I was about to move house, Hancock's enthusiasm took over.

"Here's the story," he said. "There's this Punch and Judy man, a genuine artist in his own way, with a marriage that's going wrong and a lot of bastards on the council out to nail him. ..." It hardly seemed the international subject he had been seeking so long and so hard, but by midnight as the drinks grew bigger and rain hammered the windows the outline looked firmer, the idea seemed sound.

I went away and wrote an extended treatment and within a fortnight of first talking over the project we started to frame the script. Everything, it seemed to us, revolved around a central character, the Punch and Judy man himself, and the first job was to put flesh on his bones. We christened him Wally Pinner and gave him a background. This was not germane to the film itself, but for us it helped to make him three-dimensional. He was in his mid-thirties, we decided; old enough to have served in the last war and young enough to have formed a permanent distaste for most forms of authority. He had been married for ten years and his love for his socially ambitious wife had been hammered into a kind of glum acceptance. Politically he was uncommitted, but without doubt he was anti-Tory (Edwardian father-figures such as Harold Macmillan, the then Prime Minister, were not for him). In an affluent society infested by snobs and status-seekers he was a genial outlaw. He did not warm to slogans and his personal code of conduct was something that sprouted as indomitably as a dandelion.

Certainly, his roots went deep and as the story developed he took

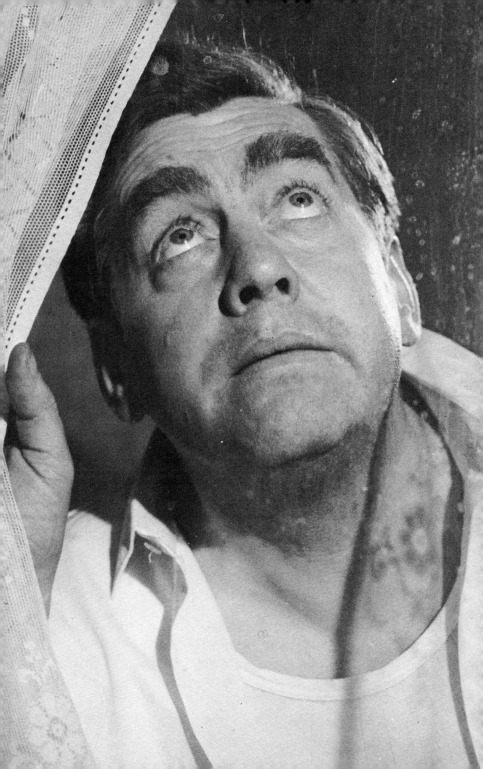

on substance. What we wanted to show was how he reacted to a moment of crisis which affected his job, his marriage, his entire future. He was no hero, but he did not go under. "He just does the best he can," said Hancock. "That's all any of us can do."

The writing of the script hung fire while Hancock went to New York for the American première of *The Rebel*. The distributors there had re-christened the film *Call Me Genius*, a title which may have helped to provoke one of the most savage receptions ever accorded to an imported comedy. Hancock found the experience so unnerving that he decided not to fly back to London – where he was convinced half Fleet Street would be waiting to grill him about the American fiasco – but to go instead to Paris where I was to join him to resume work on *The Punch and Judy Man*.

We rented a separate room in the hotel as an office, stocked it with Vichy water and typing paper, and tried – seriously tried – to get down to writing. All in vain. Hancock had been badly shaken by the New York experience and he needed time to both relax and recover. Relaxation came first. We ate a lot and drank even more. We played pin-ball (Hancock insisted on machines which had flippers to spin the ball). We walked and bought books. We continued drinking and on the third day my liver rebelled. Hancock agreed to return home but, still suspecting a hostile press reception, insisted on cancelling our air tickets and entrained to Calais where we took a boat to Dover. Mysteriously, a cabin had been reserved where champagne on ice awaited us and we first saw the white cliffs through a sentimental haze of Dom Perignon.

My wife was waiting to drive us home (we had by this time moved to Kent), but by the time we arrived there after several stops at pubs on the way, it was nearly midnight and bucketing down with rain. Hancock's home – MacConkey's – was forty miles away in Surrey. We tried to persuade him to stay the night, but he insisted on phoning for a cab. My house was in a fairly remote stretch of country and I was uncertain whether any driver could be persuaded to make the journey. Hancock, however, had no doubts. "Use the name," he said, and I did. "The taxi's for Mr Hancock," I said and within fifteen minutes the taxi was at the door and Hancock was homeward bound.

What struck me as so remarkable – both then and now – was that
the taxi-driver who answered the summons at no time asked *which*

Mr Hancock wanted to use his cab. He was not psychic. He had no private information. It was simply that for him there *was* no other Hancock. Millions of other people, I realised, felt the same way. And I was suitably impressed and daunted.

The script took us six weeks to write. For a while we rented a suite in the White House on the edge of Regent's Park. Most mornings we hit our stride by ten o'clock, only a little distracted by the demolition men across the road who spent the entire day knocking down houses by clouting them with a big steel ball suspended from the tip of a crane. Some afternoons we visited the Zoo, where I had made a series of films on animal behaviour with Desmond Morris, and spent hours on end hooting softly at the chimpanzees. It's the most basic form of animal communication (but one which never fails to impress non-animal people) and Hancock was enthralled.

Finally we moved back to MacConkey's, where the script was completed. It was not, perhaps, the most sensible move. As the story developed it became apparent that the part of it which dealt with the Punch and Judy man's marriage was bitterly and increasingly auto-biographical. The opening sequence of the film, fifteen minutes long, showed Wally and his wife (played by Sylvia Syms) at breakfast. There's no conversation. The silence is punctuated by the crunching of toast, the popping of cereal, the crackling of newspaper – all normal sounds but heightened to infuriate the person across the table. "It's about mutual hatred," said Hancock approvingly. He was describing the home life of Cicely and himself.

It was difficult, however, for me to remain outside the conflict. I liked Cicely and admired the way in which she made everything (including whatever emotional stresses there were) secondary to the job in hand. She was a beautiful red-headed girl, an excellent cook who provided food and drink and deliberately removed herself from the scene during working hours. In her way she was a good deal more professional than Hancock. She knew what was demanded of her and she did not back down.

Hancock, however, required coaxing. The day began at 8.30 a.m. when I would urge Hancock out of bed. An hour later he would present himself at the office, where I would be re-typing the previous day's work, and sit moodily in a corner. The collaboration took the form of my showing him the rough sketch of a scene I had pre-pared and then trying to provoke his reactions. Sometimes they were

enthusiastic. He was a generous man when he found something funny. At other times they were chilling.

He would hand the pages back, shaking his head. "It doesn't work."

"Why not?"

"Christ knows. We need something *more*."

"OK. But what?"

"Something funny."

"Such as ... ?"

"Something that shows what's going on between them."

"You think *that's* funny?"

"It could be."

And often it was. At his best, Hancock was a brilliant creator of comic business, and the breakfast-table sequence is, at times, inspired. Delia, his wife in the film, is an avid reader of gossip columns and her wifely ministrations are conducted blindly behind columns of newsprint. She pours the tea and Hancock has to manoeuvre his cup smartly to catch the flow. She tips out his cereal, oblivious to the fact that a plastic submarine has also bounced on to his plate. She insists on him folding his table napkin neatly (a task which Hancock would, in any case, have found impossible to perform). Furiously he leaves for work (they live above a seaside gift shop) and vents his rage by ramming a spray of artificial flowers into a plaster pig on the shop counter.

Originally the flowers were to be inserted in the pig's snout. "It's not strong enough" said Hancock. "They have to go up its arse." And so a specially designed pig was constructed to fortify the jest.

The film was largely based on his childhood memories of Bournemouth and, whatever its shortcomings, it does have the tang of salty, chapped nostalgia which comes close to our original intentions. Hancock had clear recollections of his childhood heroes, the greatest of them being the Sandman – a beach sculptor who created tableaux such as The Death of Nelson – in sand. His art (a word forever on Hancock's lips) was forever at the mercy of high tides, small children, and dogs. In the film he was played to wincing perfection by John Le Mesurier, a close friend of Hancock's from television days, as were most of the cast, which included Hugh Lloyd, Ronald Fraser, Barbara Murray, and Norman Bird. On paper it looked decidedly hopeful. But

from the first day of actual shooting at the ABPC Studios at Elstree

Flowers for a purpose-built pig

the atmosphere soured.

Hancock had been offered his choice of director. At one time – to everyone's trepidation – he talked of directing the film himself. But eventually he settled on Jeremy Summers, a young and technically adroit director, experienced in television but lightweight for the job of coping with a star whose unpredictable changes of mood could paralyse a film set. To make matters worse Hancock had decided that, in some way, the ABPC management was out to bilk him. Nothing could have been further from the truth. *The Punch and Judy Man* was to have been the first of four Hancock films made by Hancock's own production company, MacConkey Films, with ABPC backing and distribution. There were contractual wrangles (which every film-maker expects), but in Hancock ABPC saw a money-spinner and the word went out to give him his head.

The tactic failed. Hancock resented the most tentative suggestions to broaden the script (a point of view with which I wholly concurred), and when a senior executive of ABPC was delegated to try and persuade him to be more flexible he insisted on thrashing the whole matter out in his dressing room over several bottles of brandy. The discussion ended as Hancock had planned. The executive passed out, defeated. But Hancock was left with such a severe hangover that he was practically unable to work the next day.

Most of the film was shot on location at Bognor Regis, a town which – to Hancock – epitomised all that was pretentious and laughable about the English seaside. He finally settled on it after hearing the apocryphal story of how, when King George V was dying, he was promised that in the event of his recovery he would be taken to Bognor to recuperate. "Bugger Bognor," the monarch is alleged to have replied. Hancock liked that.

He also liked the inconsequential comedy of a notice he saw in the window of a mechanical grab in an amusement arcade in which the goodies on display were hopefully seized by the trunk of a metal elephant. "In the event of winning," said the notice, "ring for Ali (the mechanic in the brown coat)." The volcano which erupted every twenty minutes behind glass in the restaurant of a holiday camp further down the coast also gave him a good deal of pleasure when it was explained to him that that lava flow actually comprised Puffed Wheat forced through a nozzle by compressed air.

Filming *The Punch and Judy Man* at Elstree Studios. A free hand, but a sense of doom

His drinking, though, became heavier. And, inevitably, his work suffered. As a reaction comic – one whose comedy is basically a reaction to a line or a situation – Hancock relied to a large degree on his marvellously mobile face which could register more acutely than any dialogue degrees of rage, stupefaction, incredulity, outrage, or joy; his entire repertoire of feeling. Alcohol stiffened the muscles and slowed down his reflexes. What had been volatile became wooden. The great French photographer, Henri Cartier-Bresson, had planned to cover the making of the film and spent several days with Hancock. They clearly liked each other and Hancock was in awe of Cartier-Bresson. ("It's like being photographed by Rembrandt," he told me.) But it soon became apparent that what Cartier-Bresson was seeing through his view-finder was as depressing as the film rushes which we watched with mounting dismay night after night. As an actor Hancock had presence and sympathy. But he was not being funny.

We overhauled the script again and again. The fault, as far as we could tell, was not in the lines. The situations, especially those worked out by Hancock, had great potential. When he described them, when he acted them out, his audience would fall about with laughter. But in front of the camera the comedy died.

He was quarrelling bitterly with Cicely. They fought physically and Cicely, who had some knowledge of judo, gave as good as she got. Hancock bought her an emerald ring. But, as he gloomily related: "It's an unlucky stone. I should have known better." He looked for a scapegoat and found it in the figure of Punch, the embodiment of old evil, the libido, the malevolent mocker. Hancock attached whichever label suited him best. "The film's jinxed," he declared boozily one evening. "*He* won't let it succeed."

Shooting was eventually completed. Hancock had signed up to do a new series for Independent Television and he retained me as script consultant. But, without any discussion, he commissioned writers and scripts which I thought were below par. The original plan for MacConkey Films had been for us to produce original subjects, but Hancock was either unwilling or unable to discuss any projects. I sent him the outline of a film tentatively entitled *The Courier* in which he would play the heir to a run-down travel agency reduced to promoting out-of-season mystery trips around Britain, so that Hancock might find himself in Scunthorpe or Grimsby in mid-winter

Punch and Judy: Hancock saw the film as a comment on his marriage with a mixed coach-load of priests from the Vatican and oil million-aires from Texas. It was an opportunity, I suggested, for some fairly mordant observations on the British Way of Life. Hancock disagreed and I resigned.

The ITV series went ahead and, beginning with a viewing audience of nearly eight million, dropped to five million within three weeks. By the end of January 1963 it was out of the television Top Twenty. *The Punch and Judy Man* was released to coincide with the TV series and was generally slated by the critics, although *The Times* liked it and compared Hancock with W. C. Fields. It was small con-solation. The film has subsequently been screened several times on television and the TV Film Guides are fairly unanimous that it con-tains large chunks of vintage Hancock.

Personally, I find it sad viewing – flashes of real brilliance, moments of supremely truthful acting, but all of it shadowed by the promise of what might have been. No one can be wholly absolved from blame for the disaster. The script and the direction should have been more positive, the laughs more frequent. But the film represents a crisis in Hancock's personal and professional life; in fact, two crises which happened to coincide. And, given all the circumstances, the result was inevitable.

Professionally, Hancock and I had parted company. But when we met there was affection on both sides and always talk of the next film we would make together. One day we met in Fleet Street. I was on my way to Savile Row to be fitted for a suit and Hancock insisted on coming with me. The tailor's was one of those establishments – with brown lino floors and fitting rooms curtained in green baize – which probably spark a nostalgia in the British for the rigours they endured at public school, and – predictably – Hancock was intrigued. He watched, fascinated, as the tailor ripped off the loosely basted sleeves of the jacket and chanted the praises of Donegal tweed and worsted suitings through a mouthful of pins.

"We've got to use it in the next film," he said when we were back in the street. And he paused in mid-stride. "Does he ever swallow those pins?" he enquired hopefully.

The end down under

Over the next five years Tony Hancock performed an extended act of professional suicide. He was divorced by Cicely and married his publicist Freddie Ross, who has described their life together in a book on which she collaborated with David Nathan (*Hancock*, published by William Kimber, 1969).

For one season he performed as Master of Ceremonies for an ITV summer variety show from Blackpool. Frequently he forgot his lines, dismissing his forgetfulness with a fairly accurate prediction of what was to come next on the programme: "Just the usual lot of old rubbish." Amazingly, he topped the bill at the London Palladium and

Hancock marries his publicist, Freddie Ross; a wedding day portrait

found that the public still loved him. He appeared in two films – *The Wrong Box* and *Those Magnificent Men in Their Flying Machines*, in which his costume was enhanced by a large and genuine plaster cast on one leg. He had sustained what is known as a Pott's Fracture and although the injury was painful he relished its description.

His drinking was out of control, but he would never acknowledge the fact that he was an alcoholic. The word was abhorrent, although he knew that his condition was chronic. He made a series of TV commercials for the Egg Marketing Board with Patricia Hayes and for a few heavily sponsored seconds his genius blazed brightly enough to remind his audience what was at risk and what was soon to be totally extinguished.

There were desperate attempts to salvage what remained. One day I was telephoned by Bernard Delfont's office and asked to attend an emergency meeting (held for some extraordinary reason in the manager's office of the Odeon, Leicester Square). What did I think,

Going to work on an egg. A TV commercial made with Patricia Hayes   89

**Left: at the London Palladium.
Above: rehearsing cabaret**

I was asked, of an idea which Hancock had proposed for a production of *King Lear* with Wilfred Lawson as Lear and Hancock as the Fool? The suggestion was not altogether new. In his cups, Hancock had often mooted such a show and – without having to finance it – the notion was dangerously appealing.

Lawson – a magnificent, if erratic actor – was also a drinking man and the thought of two such performers together on stage was exhilarating, but even more terrifying for the prospective backer. Hancock also wanted Nicol Williamson – a handy man with a bottle, in his time – to join the cast. If the plan had ever matured it would have been a short run but a hectic one. Sad to say, the consensus was against it.

There was also a proposal to star Hancock in a Galton and Simpson musical based on André Obey's play, *Noah*, with a Leslie Bricusse score and sets designed by Sean Kenny. Galton and Simpson were against Hancock's involvement from the start. They knew his aversion to long runs, and the fact that the show would have cost £100,000 to stage and run for at least a year before making any profit made the project still-born.

Equally abortive was Hancock's Hollywood trip to star in a Walt Disney comedy entitled *Bullwhip Griffin* in which he was to play an Edwardian Shakespearean actor out West. His costume, ironically, was to have been the long-abandoned Homburg hat and the coat with the astrakhan collar. But one day at the studio Hancock collapsed – stress, and heat prostration, rather than drink were suggested as the cause – but the Disney lawyers pressed for cancellation of the contract. Obviously they suspected the worst, although there's no doubt that Hancock was fighting valiantly to stay off the booze. For some of the time he succeeded, although one British actor in Hollywood at the time recalls the door in his hotel being pounded at three o'clock in the morning and finding Hancock in the corridor on his knees. "I looked down at him and he looked up at me and said, 'Teach me how to act, master.' I felt like weeping to see such a good man and a great talent being destroyed."

But Hancock never quit. In September 1966 he booked the Festival Hall in London for a one-man show. "The Lad Himself Will Entertain You" said the advertisements, and he tried to live up to them. Most of the show inevitably comprised the tried-and-tested

material – the cod Shakespeare, Charles Laughton impersonations,

The film Hancock never made. On the set of *Bullwhip Griffin*

all Hancock's old reliables. But he also acted out part of *The Blood Donor* (with prompt boards in the wings) and – as always – the audience responded with love. The show was filmed by the BBC and eventually transmitted by BBC2 – a loyal but disastrous gesture. The man on the screen did not match the viewers' memory of their greatest clown, an unpalatable truth underlined by his next series for ITV, which reeled from calamity to catastrophe with Hancock as the proprietor of a wholly unbelievable night-club, grumpily linking a string of variety acts. It was both trite and pathetic. All over the land viewers switched off by the million.

There was, about Hancock, an air of impending tragedy. It was sensed by all his friends (and what was striking was how many *remained* his friends), but whatever gesture they made, it seemed that nothing could be done to avert it. Spike Milligan devised a television format which would reconcile Hancock with Galton and Simpson. "There'd be this opening sequence," he told me. "Hancock walking down the street in his Homburg and astrakhan coat and ringing Galton and Simpson's bell. 'Just thought I'd give you lads another chance,' he says. 'Let bygones be bygones.'" But it came to nothing. Gerald Thomas, director of the phenomenally successful *Carry On* series of films, proposed a movie which reunited Hancock and Sid James. James was all for it. But Hancock said no.

I remembered the press conferences at which he announced the making of *The Punch and Judy Man* and the formation of MacConkey Films. It was a big-deal evening: big drinks, big cigars. Hancock was making a number of declarations which I thought promised considerably more than we could possibly deliver and I hissed into his ear, "What's got into you? Megalomania?" He tapped the ash from his cigar and smiled blandly. "Just a touch," he agreed. But by now it was nothing so simple.

In March 1968 he went to Australia to film a series of thirteen programmes in which he was to star as the classic Hancock hero (Homburg-hatted, astrakhan-collared) setting foot on antipodean soil as a passage-assisted immigrant and instantly at odds with the Australian way of life. He was accompanied by Michael Wale, a young British writer who was to script the series. His view of Australia (as Wale recalled in an article in *The Times*) was established within a page of the opening script. Looking over the ship's rail he declares: "Of course, we Hancocks always have been a seafaring race. If it hadn't been a question of time I'd have sailed across single-handed. But life's too short to fit everything in. It's all right for Sir Francis Chichester. But I've got too much on me plate. I've got to help build a new country. After all, Captain Cook didn't arrive single-handed, did he? ... I wonder if Matilda's still waltzing around with that kangaroo?"

Inevitably, Hancock was under stress. On 21st June in London Hancock's wife, Freddie, obtained a decree *nisi*. He was again drinking heavily and he had been warned that unless he remained sober

LON-3) SYDNEY, June 25.(AP) British comedian Tony
ancock was found dead in his apartment here today.
olice said they believed he died from an overdose
f sleeping tablets.   This picture of Hancock was
ade during the shooting of a television series in
ustralia recently. (AP Wirephoto)(vh25/6/68cable)

in the studio the series would be cancelled. He tried his best to obey orders and, for a while, seemed to rally. Three episodes in the series were filmed and, says Michael Wale, "the studio used to fill with technicians on the Fridays and Saturdays that we filmed, just to admire his work".

One day he went back to his flat in a Sydney suburb after rehearsing episode four and the next morning he was found dead. The verdict was suicide: barbiturates washed down with vodka. There were two farewell notes. "Things seemed to go wrong too many times," he wrote.

I heard the news with an awful sadness, but with no surprise. All that day people asked me, "But *why* did he do it? What went wrong?" And we all found our own answers. Pride came into it, I think. Hancock was the very best there was. His talent was prodigious and to see it dwindling, becoming stale and second-rate must have been, for him, intolerable.

When I think of him now it is with love and exasperation and pride, and a sense of loss that has in no way diminished. I think of him after a sober working day, clinking the ice in his glass and murmuring, "Listen to that . . . the best sound in the world." I think of him sifting his anthology of unforgivable sayings and coming up with the winner – the prim, disapproving refusal: "Not for *me*, thank you." And I think of him standing one night in the pouring rain, lightning sizzling overhead, and some malevolent, unbelieved-in God threatening doom with peal after peal of thunder.

Hancock, the indomitable, mopped his face and looked heaven squarely in the eye. "Go on," he dared the Almighty. "Make it worse."